# FIRST PEOPLES
# THE MOHAWKS
## OF NORTH AMERICA

# CONNIE ANN KIRK

Lerner Publications Company • Minneapolis

**First American edition published in 2002
by Lerner Publications Company**

Published by arrangement with Times Editions

**Lerner Publications Company**
A division of Lerner Publishing Group
241 First Avenue North
Minneapolis, MN 55401 U.S.A.

Website address: www.lernerbooks.com

Series originated and designed by
**Times Editions**
An imprint of Times Media Private Limited
A member of the Times Publishing Group
1 New Industrial Road, Singapore 536196

Website address: www.timesone.com.sg/te

Series editors: Margaret J. Goldstein, Ng Li San
Series designers: Tuck Loong, Sandy Sum
Series picture researcher: Susan Jane Manuel

**Library of Congress Cataloging-in-Publication Data**
Kirk, Connie Ann.
The Mohawks of North America/ by Connie Ann Kirk.
p. cm. — (First peoples)
Includes bibliographical references and index.
ISBN 0-8225-4853-4 (lib. bdg. : alk. paper)
1. Mohawk Indians—Juvenile literature. [1. Mohawk Indians.
2. Indians of North America.]  I. Title. II. Series.
E99.M8 K57 2002
974.7'0049755—dc21                          00-012665

Printed in Singapore
Bound in the United States of America
1 2 3 4 5 6—OS—07 06 05 04 03 02

# CONTENTS

# THE MOHAWKS—
# A PROUD NATION

The Mohawks are a large Native American, or Indian, nation based in the northeastern woodlands of North America. The Mohawks are part of a group of native nations called the Iroquois League. Mohawk lands traditionally stretched from the Mohawk Valley in New York north to the St. Lawrence River along the Canadian border. After the American Revolution (1775–1783), many Mohawks were resettled in reservations in the United States and Canada. The modern Mohawk people do not officially recognize the boundaries placed on their lands by the U.S. and Canadian governments.

## In the United States

In the United States, large Mohawk communities live near the Mohawk River in central New York; near Plattsburgh in northern New York; at the St. Regis Reservation, at New York's border with Quebec and Ontario; and in Brooklyn, a borough of New York City. Mohawk people first moved to Brooklyn in the late 1800s, to take jobs on construction projects in New York City. At the St. Regis Reservation, the Mohawks have developed schools and other facilities to improve people's lives.

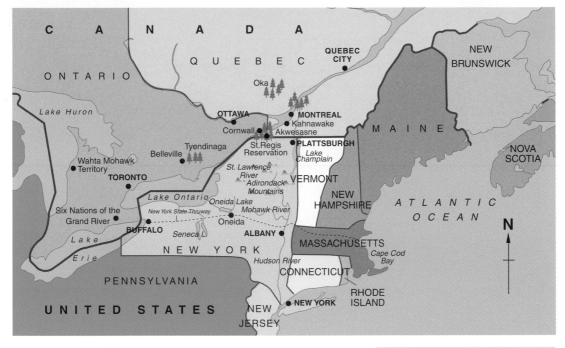

## In Canada

In Canada, Mohawk people live mostly in the provinces of Quebec and Ontario. Some Canadian Mohawks live on reservations, which are called reserves in Canada. The largest Mohawk reserve in Quebec is Kahnawake, located southwest of Montreal, a big city in Quebec. A smaller reserve called Kanesatake, or Oka, is located northwest of Montreal. In Ontario, the largest Mohawk reserve is called the Six Nations of the Grand River. The reserve's residents include Mohawks and members of the other Iroquois nations. Many Canadian Mohawks also live in Tyendinaga near Lake Ontario and in the Wahta Mohawk Territory in western Ontario.

### DISPUTED TERRITORY

In the 1950s, the U.S. and Canadian governments built the St. Lawrence Seaway, a project that connected the Great Lakes and the Atlantic Ocean. Construction destroyed traditional Mohawk fishing areas. Pollution from factories built along the seaway killed fish and wildlife. In recent years, the Mohawks have struggled with the U.S. and Canadian governments over rights to their ancestral waters and homelands. One disputed territory is Akwesasne, a large region that includes the St. Regis Reservation.

# THE SIX NATIONS

In the late 1500s, five Indian nations— the Senecas, the Cayugas, the Onondagas, the Oneidas, and the Mohawks—formed the Iroquois League. They called themselves Haudenosaunee, or People of the Longhouse, after a type of Native American dwelling. The Iroquois is another name for the group. In 1722, the Tuscaroras joined the league, which then became the Six Nations.

*Above:* The northeastern woodlands

## Special Names

Each Iroquois nation had a special name in the league, depending on where the group lived. The Senecas lived in the westernmost part of Iroquois lands and were called the Keepers of the Western Door. The Cayugas lived on marshy lands around Cayuga Lake and were called the People at the Mucky Land. The Onondagas were called the People of the Hills and the Keepers of the Council Fire. They ran the council

*Above:* A 1771 map of Iroquois lands

meetings, which were held where they lived—in the hills around Onondaga Lake. The Oneidas were called the People of the Standing Stone because of a great stone found where they lived. The Tuscaroras came to the region from North Carolina. Called the Shirt-wearing People, they used the hemp plant to make clothing and medicine.

## People of the Flint

The Mohawks called themselves Kahnyenkehaka, or People of the Flint, because they lived in a place with a lot of flint (a kind of rock). They were also called the Keepers of the Eastern Door because they lived at the eastern edge of Iroquois lands. Starting in the 1600s, European settlers arrived in North America from the east. The Mohawks, as gatekeepers and members of the large, strong, and well-organized Iroquois League, played an important role in dealings with the Europeans.

*Below:* The Mohawks guarded the easternmost part of Iroquois lands.

## Leaving Their Marks on the Map

All the Iroquois groups still live on or around their native homelands. Many towns, counties, lakes, and other places in the Northeast bear the names of these groups. For instance, Oneida is the name of a county, a town, and a lake in New York. Seneca Lake and Cayuga Lake are two of New York's long and thin Finger Lakes. Native American folklore tells how the Creator—the spirit that created the world—placed a hand on the land and left fingerprints there, making the lakes.

### THE IROQUOIS TRAIL

The modern New York State Thruway, a highway connecting the cities of Albany and Buffalo, runs almost directly over the course of a long footpath used centuries ago by Iroquois League members. Called the Iroquois Trail, the path crossed many streams, meadows, and woods. The trail linked all the Iroquois nations together. People used it to trade with each other, visit relatives, gather for council meetings, and send messages. Signs located in rest stops along the thruway educate modern travelers about the long and important history of this trail.

# THE LUSH WOODLANDS

The northeastern woodlands of North America are filled with lush forests, streams, rivers, hills, and fields. There are four distinct seasons here, with very different kinds of weather. The look of the landscape changes with each season. Rainfall is plentiful, particularly in spring and summer, and snowfall can be heavy in winter.

## Blowing Hot and Cold

Winters are often snowy and cold in the northeastern woodlands, with temperatures sometimes falling below 0 degrees Fahrenheit (-18 degrees Celsius). Springtime brings warmer weather and sunny skies, as well as lots of rain. In the midsummer months of July and August, the weather can be very hot and muggy. In fall, when the sun sits low in the sky, trees lose their leaves, and nights can be very cold.

*Left:* The Adirondack Mountains

## Highs and Lows

The landscape of northeastern North America is also varied. The Adirondack Mountains rise north of the Mohawk Valley. Rocky gorges and deep crevices are found in the Finger Lakes region. Small streams bubble over rocks and waterfalls toward large rivers and lakes in Ontario. Flat valleys and fields lie among the hills, with dark and rich soil that's good for farming. With each change of season, the landscape can take on a new and very different look.

Above: Winter transforms the woodland landscape.

## THE MOHAWK VALLEY

The beautiful and fertile Mohawk Valley is the ancestral homeland of the Mohawk people. The valley provided the Mohawks with all the essentials. The forests gave people trees for building shelter and fires. The rich soil of the fields yielded good harvests of corn, beans, and squash. The rain and streams offered water for drinking and cooking. The Mohawks traveled by canoe on the region's lakes and rivers to visit friends and relatives and to trade.

# Spectacular Colors

The trees of the region include elms, birches, maples, ashes, pines, and hickories. Ferns, grapevines, and wild berries grow on the forest floor. Wildflowers and sweet grass grow in the fields. The bright colors of the leaves in fall remind people of the colorful clothes and beading once worn by the region's native peoples. Perhaps this is why some nonnative people call a warm spell in autumn an "Indian summer."

Left: Leaves turn shades of red and gold in autumn.

# WOODLAND WILDLIFE

The northeastern woodlands are full of wildlife. Many of the animals here grow thick fur for protection in cold winters. They shed this fur in the warmer months to stay cool. Some animals have sharp teeth, which help them kill prey, build shelters, and chew through branches to reach food. Many animals have brown or black fur, which allows them to hide from their enemies by blending in well with dark soil, rocks, and tree trunks.

## White-Tailed Deer

White-tailed deer are plentiful in this region. A male deer is called a buck, and a female is called a doe. Coarse brown hair that lies flat covers the deer's body, with white hair underneath the tail. Males grow wide antlers with up to eight points, or prongs. Young deer, or fawns, often have white patches that fade to brown as the animals get older. A white-tailed deer's tail bounces and flips up when its runs, and you can then see the white underside.

## The Largest Animals

The largest mammals of the woodlands are moose and bears. Moose are larger and darker in color than deer. The males grow very large antlers, which they shed each year. It is not unusual to find the antlers lying in the woods. The black bear is the most common kind of bear in this region. Its dark brown fur often catches on branches in the woods during the shedding season. Black bears have large claws, which they use when they hunt for food.

*Left:* The moose has dark fur and a wide snout.

*Above:* Squirrels can be found in the northeastern woodlands.

*Below:* The white-tailed deer gets its name from the white fur on the underside of its tail.

# Smaller Inhabitants

Smaller animals, including beavers, rabbits, and squirrels, also live in the northeastern woodlands. Beavers use their sharp teeth to cut down trees and branches, which they use to build lodges and dams in lakes and streams. The beavers' stiff, flat tails help them stand while they work. Rabbits have silky brown fur that is sometimes spotted with different colors. Squirrels are often gray or red in color, with long furry tails. They keep busy each autumn gathering and storing nuts for the winter.

## ALMOST A NATIONAL SYMBOL

Wild turkeys (*right*) live in the northeastern woodlands. They can grow to be quite large and can fly short distances. European settlers and Native Americans feasted on wild turkeys at the first Thanksgiving celebration. Modern people eat turkeys raised on farms. Benjamin Franklin, the early American statesman and inventor, once suggested the turkey as the national bird of the United States, but the bald eagle won this honor instead. Bald eagles are also found in the Northeast.

# THE FIRST MOHAWKS

The first Mohawks were nomadic, always on the move from place to place, following the animals that provided their food. Gradually, the Mohawks built small farms and settlements, which gave them a home base between hunting trips.

## Crossing into the Americas

For years, historians believed the ancestors of modern Native Americans arrived from Asia about 15,000 years ago, by walking across the Bering Land Bridge. This strip of land connected Asia to North America thousands of years ago and has since been covered by water. However, new research shows that early peoples could have come in many different migrations from Asia, Australia, and Europe. Some historians believe that people moved into the northeastern woodlands more than 6,000 years ago.

*Below:*
The Mohawks once relied on hunting for survival.

## A Changing Lifestyle

The first Iroquois people shared a common language and lifestyle. They lived in small bands, or groups. In the cooler months, the bands hunted game and gathered food such as nuts and wild berries in present-day New York State. In the warmer months, they followed the animal herds north to Canada. The bands had a subsistence economy, hunting and gathering only what they needed for survival. Eventually, the Iroquois lifestyle began to change. In addition to hunting and gathering, people started to grow their own food. They made farms and built permanent shelters and villages. They also traded with neighboring groups. As the bands settled into villages, they became more independent of one another. Gradually, the Iroquois people separated into independent nations, such as the Mohawks.

# Making Peace

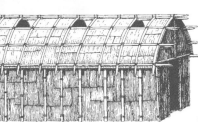

*Above:* The longhouse was the symbol of the Iroquois League nations—the Senecas, Cayugas, Onondagas, Oneidas, and Mohawks.

*Below:* Before the Great Peace, the Iroquois nations fought one another for control of the land.

For many years after the Iroquois nations settled into villages, they fought one another for control of the land. Finally, to stop the fighting, the Senecas, Cayugas, Onondagas, Oneidas, and Mohawks formed the Iroquois League in the late 1500s. The Iroquois people lived in dwellings called longhouses. The league members imagined a giant longhouse that connected the lands of all five nations, with a door at each end—a symbol of the league's unity. The Mohawks were the Keepers of the Eastern Door. The alliance brought about a long period of peace and cooperation, known as the Great Peace.

## THE GREAT PEACE

According to Iroquois legend, a Huron Indian called the Peacemaker and an Onondaga man named Hiawatha—both living among the Mohawks—convinced all five nations to form a peace agreement. The nations buried their weapons beneath the Tree of Peace, and the Iroquois League was born. The league had a federal government. Each nation kept its independence but sent representatives to league meetings to make decisions together for the benefit of all. The organization of the Iroquois League later became a model for the U.S. government.

# THE COMING OF THE EUROPEANS

The Mohawks had long traded with the other Iroquois groups. When European explorers and settlers came to the Iroquois League's "eastern door" in the 1600s, they brought tools and other goods to trade for beaver furs, which were stylish back in Europe. Trade with the Europeans changed the lives of North America's native peoples forever.

## The Beaver Trade

Beaver furs were a luxury in Europe, used to make hats and other fashionable clothing. Fur traders received a high price for them. The Mohawks exchanged beaver furs with Dutch fur traders for European goods and wampum (highly prized strings of beads). Once the Mohawks started trading with the Europeans, they killed all the beavers on their own land. They then began hunting beavers on lands of other native peoples—people who also wanted to trade furs with the Europeans. Fights over the animals led to a series of battles between native groups.

*Right:* Native Americans traded beaver furs for tools and other useful items.

# First Taste of Gunfire

*Above:* The Mohawks experienced their first gunfight in 1609.

While the native peoples fought one another for beavers, groups of Europeans in North America also fought over the land and its riches. The Europeans often asked for the help of their native trading partners in these battles. At one famous fight in 1609, the Mohawks fought against French forces and their native allies led by explorer Samuel de Champlain. The Mohawks used their traditional weapons—bows and arrows. But the opposing side fired rifles at them. Three Mohawk chiefs died that day as the Mohawks experienced their first gunfight. The Mohawks fled but did not forget their helplessness in the situation. They later traded more beaver furs for rifles of their own.

# French Influence

In their efforts to control North America, the Europeans tried to convert native peoples to Christian faiths such as Catholicism. Although the French and the Iroquois fought frequently, French missionaries, or religious teachers, were eventually allowed into Iroquois villages. The French set up churches in Mohawk and other Iroquois villages and converted some native people to Catholicism.

## KATERI TEKAKWITHA

Kateri Tekakwitha, who lived from 1656 to 1680, was caught in the struggle between native and Catholic beliefs. Her mother was a Catholic Algonquin, and her father was a Mohawk chief. She was brought up in Mohawk traditions, but at age twenty she asked French priests to baptize her. The Mohawk people treated her harshly because of her Catholic faith. Ill all her life, she died at age twenty-four. Although her face had been scarred by a disease called smallpox, the priest attending her burial claimed that her skin turned beautiful and unmarked in death. The Catholic Church honored Tekakwitha in 1980.

# THE AMERICAN REVOLUTION

I n the early 1700s, the Iroquois League was still powerful. It had strong ties to the French and to another European group fighting to control North America—the British. The French and British fought one another in a series of wars, including the French and Indian War (1754–1763). In this conflict, which the French lost, the Mohawks sided with the British and remained strong. However, the American Revolution that followed brought difficult changes for the Mohawks.

## The War of Independence

By the 1760s, American colonists (settlers) were hoping to form an independent nation in North America. Their resistance to British control led to the American Revolution (1775–1783)—the war for American independence. The Iroquois League tried to remain neutral. But some nations later supported the American colonists, while other nations, led by Joseph Brant, a Mohawk chief, backed the British.

*Above:* After the American Revolution, the British government awarded this medal to native chiefs who had supported the British during the war.

# Losing Their Land

The American colonists won the Revolution. The British lost much of their North American land, except for parts of Canada. After the war, the British government rewarded its Iroquois supporters with land in Canada. Many natives took the offer and moved from their homelands. Native people who remained in New York soon clashed with the newly formed United States government. White Americans moved onto native lands and built settlements. They took land away from the natives by force or made land treaties (agreements) that the natives could not read.

*Above:* A British general addresses native leaders during the American Revolution.

## Weakened and Divided

European activities weakened the Mohawks. Trading alliances caused them to turn against other native peoples. Divided, the Iroquois League officially ended after the American Revolution. The Mohawks were geographically split between the United States and Canada after the war. They were also divided between traditional and Christian ways. Low in both numbers and spirits, they moved to reservations and small villages, where they had little political power.

## JOSEPH BRANT: A MOHAWK CHIEF

Thayendanegea (*right*), called Joseph Brant by the British, was an educated Mohawk chief who persuaded many Iroquois warriors to fight for the British in the American Revolution. The British promised him and his Iroquois supporters protection, goods, and warm clothing in exchange for their military aid. After the war, Brant led a group of Mohawks and other Iroquois people to settle at the Grand River in Ontario, on land the British gave them.

# THE MODERN MOHAWKS

Since the American Revolution, the Mohawks have struggled to claim their rights and to remain independent within the powerful nations of Canada and the United States. The pull of modern lifestyles caused many Mohawks to abandon their traditional way of life. Many have moved off the reservations and reserves to live in large U.S. and Canadian cities. More recently, however, the Mohawks have a new appreciation for their history and culture.

## Decline of a People

Throughout the 1800s, the Mohawks suffered further loss of their lands, independence, and traditions. Missionaries continued to convert Mohawk people to Christianity. In the mid-1900s, during the construction of the St. Lawrence Seaway (connecting the Great Lakes and the St. Lawrence River with the Atlantic Ocean), more Mohawk lands were taken, treaties broken, traditional Mohawk fishing grounds destroyed, and waterways polluted.

*Right:* A young Mohawk man wears his pride on his back.

*Above:* Some present-day Mohawks still guard their land fiercely.

## Protest at Kanesatake

Even in the late 1900s, Mohawks clashed with the U.S. and Canadian governments. In 1990, Mohawks stood up to the Quebec government at the town of Kanesatake, or Oka, near Montreal. A company wanted to expand a golf course onto the site of a Mohawk burial ground there. The Mohawks staged armed protests against the project. They attracted the attention of the press and gained public support, stopping the golf course project. Although the fight has ended, the Mohawks only recently reached a settlement with the Canadian government. However, traditional Mohawks have refused to recognize the settlement.

## A Proud People Regain Their Pride

Poverty is a big problem for native peoples on most of the reservations in North America, and the Mohawks are no exception. Because few jobs are available and schools are poor, native people often lose hope. They sometimes turn to drinking, smoking, and drug use to escape their problems. In recent years, however, the Mohawks have been studying their strong and noble history. Pride is returning to Mohawk groups. Modern Mohawks are eager to rebuild their people's strength and teach young people the traditional ways of Mohawk life.

*Right:* Many Mohawks are going back to school to improve their lives.

## THE AKWESASNE FREEDOM SCHOOL: BRINGING TWO WORLDS TOGETHER

At the Akwesasne Freedom School on the St. Regis Reservation, children learn about Mohawk history and culture. Lessons are taught in the Mohawk language, except at grades 7 and 8. At those levels, lessons are conducted in English to help the children make the transition, or change, to high schools outside the reservation. Mohawk teachers have worked hard to bring their people into the twenty-first century, while at the same time keeping the traditions of their ancestors.

# ADAPTING THE OLD ECONOMY

Over the centuries, the Mohawk economy moved from hunting and gathering to farming and then to trade. Farming, hunting, and trade are still important to the Mohawk people. But they are no longer the only ways for modern-day Mohawks to earn money.

## Modern Farming

Traditionally, the Mohawks planted corn, squash, and beans. These crops are known as "the three sisters" because they grow well together. Modern Mohawk farmers still plant the three crops. Corn is especially important. Mohawk farmers sell it at local markets—by the ear or ground into meal. They also sell cornhusks, which are used as a decorative craft material. Many Mohawk farming families run roadside produce stands. They sell fresh produce to people driving by and keep some of the crop for themselves. The typical Mohawk farm does not earn enough money to support a family, so farmers must work at other jobs, too.

*Above:* Furs and feathers from woodland animals are used in many Mohawk handicrafts.

## The Hunting Industry

Hunting was important to the early Mohawks. Modern Mohawk people still hunt deer and other woodland animals. The U.S. and Canadian governments do not control hunting on Mohawk reservations as they do in other areas. As a result, some Mohawk people earn money by selling weapons to hunters, by processing deer hides and meat, and by selling furs and deerskin clothing and accessories. However, these small businesses do not usually create enough income to support a family comfortably without outside help.

## Present-Day Trade

Trade continues among the Iroquois nations and between the Mohawks and nonnative peoples. But it is a little different from the trade of the past. Instead of exchanging goods without using cash, modern Mohawk people run restaurants and shops that sell real native foods and crafts to tourists. Information about Mohawk culture is also valuable. Nonnative people want to know about the Mohawk lifestyle and will pay money for books, videos, classes, and performances to learn more about it. Sometimes the Mohawks trade with native peoples farther west, such as the Navajo and Sioux, who sell their products in Mohawk shops. In turn, Mohawk products are sold in other native peoples' shops.

## THE THREE SISTERS

The traditional practice of growing the "three sisters" of corn, squash, and beans (*left*) continues in modern Mohawk farms and gardens. Corn is planted first, in rows of small hills about 3 feet (1 meter) apart. Squash and beans are planted in the same hills, when the cornstalks begin to appear. The cornstalks support the vines of the beans. The squash helps trap moisture in the soil. The beans provide nitrogen to the soil. All the plants grow better together than they would separately.

# THE NEW ECONOMY

Modern Mohawk people, on and off the reservations, have jobs that celebrate their heritage and contribute to the societies around them. Many Mohawks are educated artists, teachers, businesspeople, and health-care workers. Mohawk people even helped build some of the tallest skyscrapers in North America, including the Empire State Building in New York City.

## Serving the Community

Since the 1900s, many young Mohawks have attended college. Many of them became teachers or doctors. Some of these professionals work in Mohawk reservations and villages, teaching and helping their own people. Mohawk lawyers often help chiefs and other nation officials write rules and other documents for governing the reservations.

## Surviving on the Reservations

On the reservations, many Mohawks run their own businesses—gas stations, restaurants, and gift shops. Shops on reservations don't have to charge sales tax. As a result, many nonnatives come to reservations to save money on products such as gasoline and tobacco. This business has been profitable for the Mohawks. Craftspeople also make baskets, carvings, and other traditional handiwork to sell to tourists as souvenirs.

*Right:* Crafts for sale in the Five Nations Iroquoian Village in Kahnawake, Quebec

# Gambling Is Big Business

Recently, many casinos have opened on Mohawk and other Native American reservations. Many nonnative people come to the reservations to enjoy the casinos, which feature gambling, dining, and entertainment. The casinos bring money to the reservations. People who come to the casinos also need to buy food, gasoline, and lodging. Many other businesses profit from the visitors. But some Mohawk people disapprove of gambling on the reservation. They say that gambling goes against traditional native ways. Other Mohawks believe gambling, like other businesses, will boost their economy and help them strengthen their communities.

*Left:* A young Mohawk craftswoman makes beadwork products.

## FEARLESS OF HEIGHTS

The Mohawks are known for being fearless when it comes to great heights (*below*). They can walk surefooted on narrow beams high in the air. Beginning in the late 1800s, construction companies paid high wages to Mohawks to help build tall buildings and bridges in big cities. Many Mohawks moved to Brooklyn, New York. They took construction jobs walking on high steel girders (support beams). Generations of Mohawk families have made their living this way.

# THE LONGHOUSE

The kanonhsehs, or longhouse, is one of the most famous features of Mohawk and Iroquois life. Modern longhouses still stand for unity within Mohawk villages and serve as places for holding council meetings and social events.

## Building a Longhouse

The typical longhouse was 20 to 23 feet (6 to 7 meters) wide and 40 to more than 200 feet (12 to more than 61 meters) long. Builders placed a series of poles into the ground in a rectangular shape to make walls. They bent saplings (thin branches) from one side of the house over to the other, making an arched roof. The roof and walls were then tied together and covered with elm bark. Holes in the middle of the roof served as chimneys for fires, which were made in pits in the middle of the longhouse floor. The longer the house, the more fire pits and chimneys it had. In bad weather, the chimney holes were covered by bark.

*Above:* A longhouse walkway was about 8 feet (2.4 meters) wide.

## Simple Interiors

Inside, the longhouse had a long open walkway. Rooms lined the walkway on both sides, one room for each family, with doors opening onto the walkway and fire pits. Walls between the rooms were made of woven fiber mats. Sleeping platforms lined the walls, high enough off the ground (about 1 foot/30 centimeters) to keep people dry. Tools and cooking utensils were also stored on platforms and in pits under the beds. Mats made of cornhusks covered the floors.

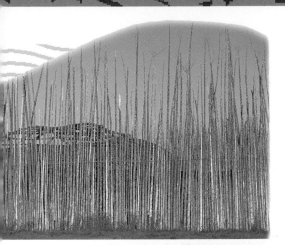

*Above:* The Mohawk village was also a fortress.

*Below:* Young boys climbed the frame of a longhouse to tie the roof and walls together. Their weight would not put too much strain on the saplings.

# Village and Fortress

In a Mohawk village, longhouses were built side by side. A log stockade surrounded the whole village. To build it, the Mohawks dug a trench about 3 feet (1 meter) deep around the village. They piled the dirt on the village side of the trench, then used logs to build a wall on top of the dirt mound. In this way, they created both a ditch and a wall that attackers had to cross before they could enter the village. A small opening in the stockade wall allowed people to walk in and out.

## THE CHANGING LONGHOUSE

Some Mohawks changed the roofs of their longhouses after the Europeans arrived in North America. Instead of the traditional arched roofs, they built triangular roofs (*above*) that resembled those on European houses. Around 1800, the Mohawks stopped building and living in longhouses altogether. They moved into houses made of wood, stone, and brick. Modern Mohawks are again building longhouses. Longhouses serve as the central meeting halls in Mohawk and other Iroquois communities. Occasionally, the Mohawk people will build a longhouse the traditional way to educate children and nonnatives about the history and structure of the longhouse.

# LIVING IN THE LONGHOUSE

In the past, extended families—parents and children, grandparents and cousins, aunts and uncles—lived together in the longhouse. Family members helped one another with basic needs, such as mending the longhouse, sewing clothing, and cooking meals. Most modern Mohawk families live in single-family houses. The longhouse is no longer used as a dwelling. Instead it serves as a place for socializing and entertaining. Mohawk families might gather at a longhouse for a picnic on a warm summer day. Council meetings, parties for winning lacrosse teams, and other events are also held at the longhouses.

# A Large Family

Mohawk society was matrilineal, meaning that kinship (family relationship) was based on the mother's side of the family. For instance, extended families in the longhouse were all related on the mother's side, and the eldest woman was the head of the household. She lived in the longhouse with her husband, her unmarried sons and daughters, and her married daughters and their husbands and children. When a man married, he moved in with his wife's parents and family. He would help extend the house that would shelter him and his wife and any children they might have. Some people believe that this practice of extending the longhouse is the basis for the expression *extended family*.

*Above:* Women played an important role in Mohawk society. The eldest women in the longhouse helped make major decisions.

## A Communal Existence

The typical longhouse had room for six to ten families—all of them related. The largest longhouses had room for twenty families. The central walkway through the house held a row of fire pits used for cooking and heating. Each family shared a fire pit with the family that lived just opposite them, in a room on the other side of the central walkway. Woven mats were hung between rooms, with storage areas for food located between one family's room and the next.

## CLANS AND DECORATIONS

The Iroquois nations were each divided into smaller groups called clans. Members of the same clan were not allowed to marry each other. There were three Mohawk clans, each named after an animal—the turtle, the bear, and the wolf. The clans were proud of their animal symbols (*right*) and often decorated their clothing and homes with them. On reservations, clan symbols are still common. They are used to decorate signs, mailboxes, and the fronts of homes and garages.

# LIFE IN THE IROQUOIS LEAGUE

Each Iroquois nation had its own rules and kept its independence. Yet the nations made many decisions together and united against enemies. The authors of the U.S. Constitution admired the Iroquois League and used it as one of the models for their own government.

## Powerful Clan Mothers

Clan mothers, the eldest women in each clan, chose the clan's sachems, or chiefs. If a chief acted poorly in his duties and did not improve, the clan mother could remove him from the job. Clan mothers also named all the newborn babies in the clan and made sure that no two living people had the same name. After someone died, his or her name was returned to the "bag of names." It could then be given to a newborn child once again. Modern Mohawks still practice this tradition.

*Above:* A Cayuga chief speaks to council members.

## The League Council

Fifty sachems from the five nations made up the council that ruled the original Iroquois League. Each nation sent a different number of sachems to council meetings, depending in part on its number of clans. The Mohawks and Oneidas each sent nine sachems, the Onondagas fourteen, the Cayugas ten, and the Senecas eight. Warriors and people who had distinguished themselves in some way could also attend council meetings. Such people were called Pine Trees. But only the sachems could vote.

# Making Decisions

Because of their central location in Iroquois territory, the Onondagas always hosted the league council meetings. They tended the fire in the league's big meetinghouse and presented the topics to be discussed by the council members. One by one, in a planned order, each nation's sachems voiced their concerns and cast their votes. Decisions had to be unanimous, meaning that everyone had to agree before action could be taken. A council of all the chiefs took place at least once a year, but chiefs sometimes met separately outside of the main council meeting.

*Below:* The kastoweh (headdress) of a sachem held antlers and large eagle feathers.

## A MODEL FOR THE UNITED STATES CONSTITUTION

Benjamin Franklin (*below*) studied the organization of the Iroquois League when he helped draw up the U.S. Constitution. The United States government has many similarities to the league. Like the league council, the U.S. Congress consists of representatives from each state. Members of Congress meet together and discuss proposals. Then they vote on whether or not the proposals should become laws for the whole country.

# THE MOHAWK FAMILY

I n the past, Mohawk family life involved unique roles for women, men, and children. In modern times, the roles of men and women in Mohawk society are less specific. Although Mohawk people no longer live in extended family groups, family ties are still an important part of Mohawk life.

## Women Ruled the Farm

In traditional Mohawk society, women tended the land. They grew and harvested crops. The women, not the men, owned the farms. Mohawk women also gathered wild nuts, such as hickory nuts and walnuts, and fruits, such as blueberries and strawberries. They tapped maple trees in spring to get sap, which they mixed with corn and other ingredients to make sweeteners for food. Modern Mohawk women generally are not farmers. They often hold jobs to earn wages, or they care for their children at home.

# Men: Not Just Warriors

Mohawk men hunted, fished, and made weapons, tools, and shelters. To capture game and fish, craftsmen made bows, arrows, wooden traps, and nets. Modern Mohawk men still hunt and fish for food, but Mohawk families usually buy food at the store, too. To support their families, modern Mohawk men work at paying jobs, mostly off the reservations.

*Left:* A modern Mohawk family

*Above:* A Mohawk man demonstrates how bows and arrows were made in the past.

# Mohawk Children

In the past, Mohawk girls helped their mothers sew clothing and make moccasins (soft leather shoes) and jewelry. Boys learned to be good hunters and warriors from their fathers and uncles. Both girls and boys learned from elders, who sat alongside them as they worked. Children learned traditional stories, songs, and dances at religious festivals in wintertime. Babies were sometimes wrapped up in cradleboards— flat boards that hung from their mothers' backs. If a mother needed to work outside, she could hang the cradleboard on a nearby tree, where the baby could see her.

## THE SEVENTH GENERATION

The Mohawks have always honored the earth, and they teach their children to tend the earth "to the seventh generation yet unborn." This saying means that the Mohawks always consider the long-term effects of their actions. Future generations will inherit the earth, and the Mohawks think about how their decisions will affect these unborn generations. The modern environmental movement often looks to native peoples like the Mohawks for good ideas about how to protect the earth's land, air, and water for future generations.

# A RICH AND BUSY LIFE

In the past, everyday life was rich and busy for the Mohawks. Houses had to be built. Food had to be caught, gathered or grown, and prepared. Clothing had to be made and mended. Disagreements also had to be resolved. Modern life is just as busy for the Mohawks, but their daily tasks have changed.

## Dressing as a Mohawk

The early Mohawks made their own clothing from deerskin and adorned it with beads. The adornments served as decoration and sometimes told a story about the wearer. The Mohawks wore kastoweh—headdresses with feathers. They made clothing out of bearskin and the fur of other animals to stay warm in winter. Moccasins were usually sewn out of deerskin, but summer shoes were sometimes made of cornhusks. Large, flat snowshoes helped people walk through deep snow without sinking. Modern Mohawks buy most of their clothing, but they often wear handmade extras like belts, belt buckles, and hats.

*Left:* Snowshoes were made from large frames of hickory crisscrossed with strips of deer hide.

## Teaching the Young

Education has always been an important part of Mohawk culture. In the past, children learned the skills necessary for survival from their parents and their clan elders. These skills included hunting, farming, cooking, and sewing. Modern Mohawk children either attend local public schools or reservation schools. At some reservation schools, children learn both traditional and modern lessons. The Mohawks hope that by educating their children in both the old and new ways of life, they can keep their culture alive and well.

## Staying Healthy

People called false-face healers cared for the health of early Mohawks. These healers wore special masks to represent different woodland spirits, each one good at curing different ailments. The masks were carved on living trees and were cut away only when they were complete. Healers also used potions and ointments made from plants to treat sickness. Modern Mohawks blend traditional cures with modern treatments. Some reservations are working to establish better health care for the people there.

## Fun and Games

The Mohawks enjoyed games and sports. Snow snake was a common winter game. Each player would throw and slide a long hickory pole as far as possible across the snow. In another game, players would tap a wooden bowl and try to turn the same colored sides of six or eight peach pits—colored black on one side and white on the other—face up.

*Left:* Traditional Mohawk clothes originally had no feathers—except on headdresses. Later, feathers were added to other types of clothing, too.

### LACROSSE: THE CREATOR'S GIFT

Lacrosse is probably the most well-known Mohawk sport. The Mohawks believed that they received the game as a gift from the Creator. In modern times, lacrosse is popular among native and non-native people. Each player uses a stick (*right*)—which has a handle on one end and a webbed pocket on the other—to catch and throw a ball. Using the sticks, players on two teams try to run the ball down a field and shoot it into the opposing team's goal. Mohawk International Lacrosse, a small family-owned business in New York, sells wooden lacrosse sticks made by Mohawk craftspeople. Lacrosse players think these sticks are among the finest.

# USEFUL AND DECORATIVE ARTS

Traditional Mohawk artwork was both decorative and useful. For instance, the Mohawks made rattles, baskets, and belts that had special uses in hunting, communication, storage, and ceremonies. Modern Mohawk people still make these items. But they are no longer made for practical use. Instead, the items are sold in shops or displayed at art shows and museums.

## Mohawk Rattles

The Mohawks made rattles from horn, elm bark, turtle shells, and dried-out gourds filled with pebbles, kernels of corn, or other small objects. The rattles were used for both hunting and ceremonies. During a hunt, hunters used rattles to frighten game, so that the animals ran where it was easiest for the hunters to kill them. In religious and social ceremonies, the Mohawks shook rattles to keep time with chants or songs.

## Handmade Baskets

The Mohawks made baskets from ash wood and sweet grass to hold corn, squash, small tools, and other items. These baskets were used to store food and materials inside longhouses or to carry crops and tools from the fields to the longhouse. The Mohawks still make baskets to use as containers. The baskets are a popular and highly valued folk art.

*Left:* A black ash and sweet grass basket

# Communicating with Wampum Belts

Originally, the Mohawks did not have a written language. Instead, they recorded information using wampum, strings of polished and colored beads made from shells. By arranging the beads into different designs,

*Below:* A wampum belt from about 1785. Wampum belts were traditionally purple and white—the colors of the shells from which they were made.

the Mohawks created pictographs, or picture symbols. To record lots of information, they sewed many strands of beads onto fabric or skin belts, called wampum belts. Many traditional wampum designs are still copied or updated. But modern wampum belts are used more for decoration than for communication. Modern Mohawk people also use a written language, created by French priests who wrote down Mohawk words using their own alphabet in the early 1700s.

*Left:* Mohawk young people make music with horn rattles and a rawhide drum.

## CONTINUING THE TRADITION

Modern museums feature Mohawk artwork from the past and the present. Non-native visitors, art collectors, and museum directors appreciate the natural materials and the fine artistry in the work. Mohawk people are happy to maintain their culture and traditions through artwork and are proud to create works that display their heritage. Using the materials and techniques of old, new Mohawk artists will leave future generations stories about their own lives and times.

# ART IN EVERYDAY LIFE

In the past, the Mohawks made decorative artwork for enjoyment, to tell stories, and to tell about the deeds of the wearer. Modern Mohawk artists carry on the traditions. They realize that their artwork appeals to nonnatives as well as natives. Sculptures and other art pieces bring high prices in galleries and are displayed in museums. In this way, the Mohawks use their skills to bring money to their villages and reservations.

*Right:* A moose antler carving in the shape of an eagle

## Antler Carvings

Mohawk carvings made on moose antlers are rare and special. Moose lose their antlers each year. Mohawk artists traditionally collected and carved them into animals and figures. The carvings were long and thin, like the antlers themselves, and often represented the spirits of the woodlands where the moose lived. When polished, the antlers were glossy white and looked like ivory.

## Cornhusk Dolls

Mohawk girls once played with dolls made of cornhusks. Some of the dolls were simple, but others were dressed up in traditional clothes and feathers. Cornhusk dolls are popular at gift shops in Mohawk villages and reservations. Small, plain dolls are usually inexpensive, but dressed-up dolls cost more.

*Left:* Some cornhusk dolls in costume are worth a lot of money to doll collectors. Doll collectors value the workmanship, the natural materials, and the way in which cornhusk dolls show aspects of Mohawk culture.

## Beads and Feathers

The Mohawks made decorative objects from beads, feathers, and quills. They made beaded shoes, clothing, and other items, with intricate designs that told stories from the past. They sewed long rows of white-and-black porcupine quills onto clothing and headdresses. They often used large eagle, turkey, and pheasant feathers to make colorful headdresses for sachems. Some headdresses worn by famous Mohawk chiefs are displayed in modern museums.

*Above:* Handmade beaded moccasins for toddlers

## TRAVELING BY CANOES

Canoes were important vehicles for the Mohawks. The Mohawks created dugout canoes (*below*) by hollowing out tree trunks. But they also traded with the Algonquin people for birch-bark canoes. Both kinds of canoes were well made and water resistant. For the Mohawks, canoeing on lakes and rivers was faster than walking through the woods, which were thick with trees and brush. Modern Mohawk people drive cars and trucks, but many still enjoy the water in boats and aluminum canoes. Occasionally, they make canoes in the traditional way—to teach people about this swift and quiet way of getting around.

# SPEAKING MOHAWK

The traditional Mohawk language was similar to other Iroquois languages. Other members of the Iroquois League could understand it. In modern times, the Mohawks lead the way among the Iroquois in saving their language from extinction.

## Keeping the Mohawk Language Alive

After Europeans came to North America, the Mohawks had to learn to speak English to survive in white society. But some people still want to speak the Mohawk language. In recent times, language classes, books, and audiotapes help teach the language to young and old. Several books and documents have been published in the Mohawk language. Websites offer help with pronunciation.

*Left:* A traffic sign in the Kahnawake Reserve, Quebec. The word *téstan* is Mohawk and *arrêt* is French. They both mean "stop."

# A Tradition of Storytelling

Storytelling has always been an important part of Mohawk life. Modern Mohawk people often visit schools to share their traditional stories with children from other backgrounds. If you were to listen to a Mohawk speaker, you'd notice a lot of "th" sounds and shorts puffs of breath in the words. You'd also hear deep low sounds that are sort of like grunts. These sounds give the Mohawk language an earthy and soothing feeling.

| | | |
|---|---|---|
| ahkwesen | (ah-kweh-SEHN) | partridge |
| awiyo | (a-WIH-yoh) | good |
| kahwatsire | (kah-HWA-tsih-reh) | family |
| kwe | (kweh) | hello |
| nia:wen | (nee-ah-wehn) | thank you |
| o:nen | (oh-nehn) | good-bye |
| o'seronni | (oh-seh-rohn-NEE) | white people |
| otara | (oh-tah-rah) | clan |
| raks'a | (rahk-SAH-ah) | boy |
| skennen | (SKEHN-nehn) | peace |
| yeksa'a | (yehk-SAH-ah) | girl |
| yonkyatenron | (yohn-kyah-TEHN-rohn) | friend |

*Above:* Some Mohawk words, their pronunciations, and their English meanings

## Learning Mohawk

A legend says that one day the Mohawks will return to their ancestral homelands and that their children will teach them their native language. This legend appears to be coming true at the Akwesasne Freedom School at the St. Regis Reservation. The children there are learning the Mohawk language and are even teaching it to their parents.

*Left:* Mohawk children and teachers at the Indian Way School, Kahnawake, Quebec

## THE STORY OF NAMES

Often, the first Europeans in North America tried to imitate words from the native languages. For example, the Algonquin people, enemies of the Iroquois, called them Irinakhoiw, meaning "real snakes." The French picked up the term, which they changed to Iroquois. Mohawk, meaning "man-eaters," is also a name given by enemies. The Mohawks called themselves by a different name—the Kahnyenkehaka, or People of the Flint. While the Mohawks were often peaceful, their reputation as fierce warriors earned them the man-eaters name. The modern Mohawks tolerate and even use this name, although it is not accurate.

# MOHAWK BELIEFS

Traditionally, the Mohawks held religious festivals to thank the Creator, or Great Spirit, for gifts from the land. Many modern Mohawks still practice the traditional religion with festivals and other rituals. Those who worship the Creator are called traditional Mohawks. Other Mohawks practice Christianity, which was introduced hundreds of years ago by French priests.

*Above:* Dream catchers were hung in the longhouse to stop bad dreams from coming true.

## The Spirit World

In the traditional Mohawk belief system, spirits called orenda inhabited the natural world and some special objects. People who seemed to be especially in tune with orenda were called the Keepers of the Faith. They were in charge of religious festivals. Dreams were another important part of Mohawk beliefs. They were said to express a person's innermost wishes and thoughts. They had to come true for the person to be at peace. The Mohawks hung rings of twigs crisscrossed with netting in the longhouse at night. These "dream catchers" captured bad dreams, so that dreamers didn't have to live them out.

## Respect for the Dead

A Mohawk funeral was called a condolence ceremony. When a Mohawk chief died, the people held a special condolence ceremony to mourn his passing and to choose his replacement. During the ceremony, a chief would recite the names of all the past Mohawk chiefs, from the chiefs of the first Iroquois League council to modern chiefs. The speech was memorized and passed by word of mouth from one generation to the next. Wampum beads and a tool called a condolence cane, marked with holes, pegs, and pictographs (small drawings), helped the chief remember all the names. At one modern-day condolence ceremony, it took more than seven hours to recite the names of all the chiefs.

*Below:* Pictographs and pegs on a condolence cane

## Religious Freedom

French missionaries first taught Christianity to the Mohawks in the 1600s. The missionaries set up religious schools. For many years, they gave lessons to Mohawk children. Many modern Mohawks still practice Christianity. But Mohawks who hold traditional beliefs don't always agree with Christian teachings. Sometimes tensions rise between the different groups. During the Great Peace, the Iroquois League made a law guaranteeing freedom of religion. Christian Mohawks say that this law protects their right to practice Christianity.

*Below:* A Christian Mohawk church

### HOW THE WORLD CAME TO BE

The Mohawk creation story is a well-known tale. According to this story, a very large tree grew in a world above this one. The tree was uprooted, leaving a big hole in the land. A woman named Sky Woman fell through the hole into our world, which was covered in water at that time. Swans caught her and stood her on a turtle's back in the water. Other animals brought up mud from beneath the water and put it on the turtle's back. The lands grew from this mud, and Sky Woman gave the world plants with seeds she had brought from above.

# A PEOPLE CELEBRATE

Most Mohawk festivals were held in the planting and harvesting seasons. Some festivals were daylong events. Others stretched for more than a day. During these festivals, the Mohawks danced, sang, and thanked the Great Spirit for the gifts of the earth. They also asked for blessings on their crops and a good harvest that would feed the people all winter. Modern Mohawks still celebrate these festivals, many of which have become part of American society.

*Above:* Buckets tied to a maple tree for collecting sap

## Spring Festivals

In early spring, the Mohawks held the Maple Festival. They thanked the Great Spirit for the arrival of spring and for the gift of "sweet waters" in the form of sap dripping from the maple trees. The trees were tapped and the sap drained into buckets. Sap was then cooked into syrup and other foods. Maple candies and syrup are still part of this festival, which also includes dancing and singing.

In late spring, the people offered songs to the Great Spirit during the Planting Festival. They asked the spirit to bless the seeds recently planted. The Mohawks hoped for plenty of rainfall and that their fields would yield a good harvest. Even though they no longer do much farming, modern Mohawks hold this festival to keep their history alive.

*Left:* Strawberries are ripe for the picking in summer.

## The Strawberry Festival

The Mohawks hold the Strawberry Festival around late May or June, about the time when small wild strawberries appear in the fields. Their appearance means that summer is on its way. In the past, the Mohawks gathered the tiny sweet fruits and ate them. They wove baskets in the shape of strawberries and painted them red with green tops. Modern Mohawks and non-Mohawks still enjoy eating strawberries. Many towns in and around the Mohawk region hold strawberry festivals, which developed from the Mohawk tradition.

## The Green Corn Festival

The Mohawks hold the four-day Green Corn Festival in August, when the "three sister" crops of corn, beans, and squash are ripe and ready to be picked. This celebration was, and still is, a grand festival that included dancing, singing, games, and blessings. As in the past, children born after midwinter are given their names during the festival. People also recite the Thanksgiving Address to offer thanks to the Great Spirit for a good crop.

*Left:* Corn is an important crop to the Mohawks. The Green Corn Festival celebrates a good harvest.

## THE THANKSGIVING ADDRESS

The Thanksgiving Address is one of the most well-known examples of Mohawk literature. Modern children learn it in both English and Mohawk. The address was originally given as a speech. In the speech, the Mohawks thanked the Great Spirit for the earth and its blessings, such as the land, water, and animals. The address shows the value that the Mohawks place on nature and how their religion is closely connected to the earth.

# FALL AND WINTER FESTIVALS

In fall, thankful for a good harvest, the Mohawks would prepare for a long, snowy winter—a time of storytelling and important meetings held inside the longhouses. The traditional fall and winter festivals celebrated the harvest and new year. Modern fall and winter festivals are mainly ceremonial, because the Mohawks no longer depend on farming to survive.

*Above:* Ripened pumpkins are a reminder that fall has come.

## The Harvest Festival

In early October, the Mohawks held the Harvest Festival. In the past, all the crops would have been picked and stored away for the winter by this time. Like the Green Corn Festival, the celebration lasted for four days. There were songs, prayers, dances, games, and feasts. People gave thanks to the "three sisters" of corn, beans, and squash. They ate a food called succotash, which contains all three ingredients. Modern Mohawks still celebrate the fall season. They fill baskets with ripened pumpkins, squashes, gourds, and other crops. They welcome many tourists, who come to the reservations and Mohawk villages to enjoy the crisp weather and the spectacular red, orange, and yellow colors of the fall leaves.

# The Midwinter Festival

The Midwinter Festival was the longest Mohawk festival of all. It lasted nine days and was held indoors in January. To begin the festival, two elders visited each home in the village to announce that a new year had arrived. They stirred the ashes of old fires in the homes and instructed the families to clean their houses and build new fires for the new year. Babies born after the Green Corn Festival received their names at this festival.

*Below:* The Mohawks would pick and store the crops for winter and celebrate a good harvest at the Harvest Festival.

## TOBACCO: A SACRED PLANT

In the past, tobacco (*above*) was a sacred plant that was burned and smoked at Mohawk festivals. Modern Mohawks still consider tobacco a sacred plant, and they still use it at festivals. However, many Mohawks who use commercial tobacco products, such as cigarettes, suffer health problems like lung cancer. Still, commercial tobacco products bring income to the reservations because they are sold there tax-free. Modern Mohawk parents try to teach their children to respect the tobacco plant as an important part of their heritage, without encouraging smoking.

# GLOSSARY

**alliance:** an agreement uniting two or more groups of people

**casino:** a facility for gambling

**ceremonial:** symbolic as opposed to practical

**condolence:** an expression of sympathy to a friend or relative of someone who has died

**crevice:** a gap or crack in the land

**extended family:** a family group that includes not just the parents and children but also cousins, aunts, uncles, and grandparents

**federal government:** a political system in which independent groups send representatives to a central governing body

**intricate:** having many small details

**kanonhsehs** (kah-NONH-sehs): an Iroquois longhouse or dwelling

**kastoweh** (kahs-toh-wee): a traditional Mohawk headdress

**matrilineal:** based on descent through the female line of the family

**migration:** a movement of people from one place to another to live or work

**neutral:** describing people or nations that do not take sides in a disagreement

**nomadic:** moving from place to place, without a permanent home

**pictograph:** a picture used to give information; a symbol

**reservation:** an area of land in the United States set aside for Native American use. In Canada, reservations are called reserves.

**stockade:** a defensive barrier made of poles driven into the ground

**subsistence economy:** a system in which people make or gather only what they need to survive

**transition:** a change from one state or position to another

**unanimous:** involving the agreement of everyone present

# FINDING OUT MORE

## Books

Bolton, Jonathan, and Claire Wilson. *Joseph Brant: Mohawk Chief.* Philadelphia: Chelsea House, 1992.

Bonvillain, Nancy. *The Mohawk.* New York: Chelsea House, 1993.

Bruchac, Joseph. *Children of the Longhouse.* New York: Penguin, 1996.

Ciment, James, and Ronald LaFrance. *Scholastic Encyclopedia of the North American Indian.* New York: Scholastic, Inc. 1996.

Gravelle, Karen. *Growing Up Where the Partridge Drums Its Wings: A Mohawk Childhood.* New York: Franklin Watts, 1997.

Lund, Bill. *The Iroquois Indians.* Danbury, CT: Children's Press, 1997.

## Videos

*Indians of North America: Iroquois.* Schlessinger Video Productions, 1993.

*More Than Bows and Arrows: The Legacy of the American Indians.* Wood, Knapp, and Co. Inc, 1995.

*Native Americans Series: Nations of the Northeast.* Turner Home Entertainment, 1994.

## Websites

<http://www.indians.org/welker/mohawk>

<http://www.ipl.org/youth/hello/mohawk>

<http://www.iroquoismuseum.org>

<http://www.peace4turtleisland.org>

<http://www.tyendinaga.net/ohenton>

<http://www.tyendinaga.net/stories/creation>

## Organizations

Akwesasne Cultural Center
Route 37
RR #1, Box 14C
Hogansburg, NY 13655-9705
Tel: (518) 358-2240 or 358-2461
Fax: (518) 358-2649
E-mail: <akwlibr@nc3r.org>

Iroquois Indian Museum
P. O. Box 7
Howes Cave, NY 12092
Tel: (518) 296-8949
Fax: (518) 296-8955
E-mail: <info@iroquoismuseum.org>

Six Nations Indian Museum
HCR 1 Box 10
Onchiota, NY 12989
Tel: (518) 891-2299

# INDEX

## ABOUT THE AUTHOR

Connie Ann Kirk is a descendant of the Seneca nation of the Iroquois League. She is a writer and scholar who lives with her husband and two sons in the Finger Lakes region of New York.

The author and the publishers would like to thank Sue Ellen Herne of the Akwesasne Museum and John Kahionhes Fadden of the Six Nations Indian Museum for their help.

## PICTURE CREDITS

(B=bottom; C=center; I=inset; L=left; M=main; R=right; T=top)

Bob Burch/Reflexion/Fraser Photos: 7C • Canadian Press: 19TL • D. Saulnier/HBL Network Photo Agency: 10–11M • David Simson: 4–5B, 11BR • Earl Kowall: cover, 4 • Hulton Getty/Archive Photos: 17B, 27T, 35T • Eastern Door/Fraser Photos: 30, 38–39M • John Fadden: 12–13T, 28L, 39T • Nazima Kowall: 32–33M • North Wind Picture Archives: 6B, 13, 14–15M, 14–15T, 16L, 16–17M, 20–21M, 29B, 42L, 44L, 44–45M • Phil Norton/Fraser Photos: title page, 2, 3, 12L, 18, 19R, 20L, 22R, 23L, 24L, 24–25M, 24–25T, 25I, 26–27M, 27BR, 28–29M, 32L, 33BR (courtesy of Kanien'kehaka Raotitionhkwa Cultural Center), 34–35M, 36L, 36–37M, 37TR, 38L, 40, 41TL, 41B, 43BL, 46 • Topham Picturepoint: 9B, 23R, 31, 34L, 37BR, 45TR • Victor Englebert: 8–9M, 10L • Winston Fraser: 6–7M, 8L, 11T, 42–43M